BALTIC Centre for Contemporary Art
ANDREW GUEST

SCALA

INTRODUCTION

Looking at BALTIC Centre for Contemporary Art across the River Tyne from its north (Newcastle) side today, it is hard to imagine that as recently as the early 1980s there were ships in the river unloading grain, coal and other goods. Or, looking along the river to the church of St Mary on the right, that in the thirteenth century (although the church may date from earlier) this was the focal point of the settlement of Gateshead (the name is variously thought to mean 'head of the [Roman] road' or 'headland roamed by goats'). Wealthy merchants built their fashionable houses in the streets around the church until the nineteenth century when they moved south, away from the (by then almost certainly smelly) river, and factories replaced the houses. In 1925 the river bank was cleared to make way for the construction of the Tyne Bridge, the green arc to the right of the church. From then this part of Gateshead, cut off from the rest of the town by new road systems and old railway tracks, went into gradual decline. The factories – which included a rope works, a gas works, iron works, chemical works, a cement factory and one of the largest locomotive works in the world – came and went, and by the Second World War had mostly disappeared for good.

The opening of BALTIC as a centre for contemporary art in 2002 is also the story of the revitalisation of Gateshead's riverside, and the renaissance of Gateshead itself. With the opening in 2001 of the Gateshead Millennium Bridge to link the town to its older and richer rival, Newcastle, and the 2004 opening of the shiny snail-like music centre known as the Sage Gateshead only yards along the river to the west, this story is also a significant chapter in the regeneration of Tyneside, and the post-industrial transformation (still very much in progress) of the whole of the North East of England.

← BALTIC viewed from Newcastle Quayside with artwork by Invader in Viewing Box

→ BALTIC viewed from Newcastle Quayside with Gateshead Millennium Bridge in the foreground

THE BALTIC FLOUR MILL

The brick building we now know as BALTIC was only one part of a large flour mill (Baltic Flour Mills) built by Joseph Rank Ltd on a vast site that extended along the river to the east of the present building and away from the river to the south. Designed in the 1930s by the Hull architects Gelder and Kitchen, the foundations were laid in the later part of that decade, although work stopped during the Second World War. The mill was only completed and started production in 1950 – ironically, just as most of the industries around it were closing. Baltic (thought to be named after the Baltic Sea by Rank, who gave his mills the names of different seas and oceans) was known locally as 'the pride of Tyneside'. At its peak, 300 people were employed on the site, which also contained storage warehouses, laboratories and a test bakery. The mill was considered to be a 'marvellous place to work' and the company provided facilities for its employees in the form of clubs, a works football team, regular outings, office parties and annual dinners, and numerous awards for good work. In 1957 the Blue Cross Mill for processing animal feeds was added. A fire in this mill in 1976 heralded falling sales and the complex was closed in 1982, although the silos (the part of the building subsequently converted into the present day BALTIC) remained open until 1984 to store part of the European Economic Community's grain mountain.

Grain was delivered by ship from countries including Canada, Australia, Chile and America, and after milling the flour was taken away by lorry to bakeries throughout the North of England. The grain travelled from the ships on a conveyor belt that ran under the wharf and was lifted up in elevator buckets to be tipped into the top of the silos. After testing the grain was withdrawn from the bottom of the

↓ *The north face of Baltic Flour Mills with ship delivering grain*

→ The original Baltic Flour Mills with Hovis sign

silos and taken to the mill. The building contained 148 of these concrete silos (each 2.5 x 2.5m²) occupying the full height of the middle four storeys of the building, with the equipment for the elevators located in the storey below and above the silos. The strength of this massive structure, which could store 22,000 tons of grain, was one reason why this part of the mill survived while the rest was demolished after its closure in 1982. The building was sold by Rank to a local property company for less than £100,000 and was later sold on to a London property company for a large profit. In the late 1980s a proposal was drawn up to convert the Baltic building into flats, but the conversion was too expensive, the owner became bankrupt and the property ended up in the hands of the receivers.

WANTED: AN ART CENTRE FOR GATESHEAD AND THE NORTH OF ENGLAND

The starting point for the story of BALTIC as a centre for contemporary art could be 29 November 1917, when the Mayor of Gateshead opened the Shipley Art Gallery in a brand new building just over a mile to the south of the town centre. Shipley was a Newcastle solicitor whose bequest of his collection of 2,500 paintings, along with £30,000 to build a gallery to house them, was rejected by the City of Newcastle but snapped up by Gateshead. It was a similar kind of opportunism in the 1980s, together with strong political leadership, the steady growth of the Council's Arts Team, the prompting and support of the regional arts association and the funding of the National Lottery, that were key factors in bringing BALTIC Centre for Contemporary Art to fruition in 2002.

In 1986, the year when Gateshead Council first established an Arts Team in its Parks and Libraries

Department, the North East of England might have seemed to many a backwater with regards to contemporary art. But from the mid 1950s, when Richard Hamilton and Victor Pasmore were teaching at Newcastle upon Tyne, the North East had been developing its very distinctive approach to the making and support of contemporary art. In 1961 the North Eastern Association for the Arts (subsequently to become Northern Arts, and now part of Arts Council England) was founded, followed by the Amber Film and Photography Collective in 1969, and Side Gallery – Stuart Brisley's 12-month Artist Placement Group residency in Peterlee – in 1976. Then came the start of the Art on the Metro programme in 1980, and in 1982 (the year when Baltic Mill closed), the founding of Projects UK. It was into this active field of multiple players, which had grown despite or because of the lack of a single major venue, that the concept of BALTIC was projected.

Gateshead first put itself on the national map as a cultural destination when it hosted the fourth UK Garden Festival from May to October 1990. Work by over 50 artists was commissioned for the festival, and in the same year Gateshead itself began work on a Sculpture Park of permanent works sited along the Tyne to the west of the Tyne Bridge. In 1993 the proposal was first mooted that culminated five years later in the construction of *The Angel of the North*, Antony Gormley's 20-metre-high Cor-Ten steel figure which quickly achieved Gateshead considerable national and international fame.

By 1990 the case for culture as a force for economic regeneration was giving new strength to the national arts funding bodies, and in its five-year plan of 1991 Northern Arts made clear its support for 'major new capital facilities for the Contemporary Visual Arts and Music in Central Tyneside'. With a push from its Libraries Department, Gateshead Council caught on to this and began looking for a site for an art centre. Despite initial reports that said the Baltic silo building was unsuitable for conversion into an art centre, and that the business case for such a venture did not stack up, interest continued, and with Northern Arts clearly favouring the idea of the conversion of an old building, Gateshead Council purchased the silo building. As a Council, Gateshead had opted out of the kind of development now beginning to take place on the opposite bank, where the Tyne and Wear Development Corporation (set up by a Conservative government in

→ *BALTIC east face with wing door*

1987), with the encouragement of Newcastle City Council, were now beginning on a fast-track plan which would see private developers create hotels, offices, restaurants and flats. Gateshead's solidly Labour-controlled council preferred to do their own thing, and with national arts cash on offer, decided to focus on providing facilities not only for their own ratepayers but that would also promote Gateshead as a cultural venue on the national and international stage. With funding from Northern Arts a feasibility study was completed, and in 1994 the Council invited the Royal Institute of British Architects to run an open competition to find an architect to convert the Baltic building into an art centre.

THE BRIEF

The Arts Brief for the competition was simple yet ambitious. It opened with: 'Our objective in the development and conversion of Baltic Flour Mills is to provide a national and international centre for contemporary visual arts with large temporary exhibition spaces. Both in scale and in artistic policy it would be unique in this country and one of only half a dozen comparable facilities in the world.' The brief cited a number of comparable projects across the globe, including the recent conversion of a flour mill in Oporto, Portugal, into a contemporary gallery, and the Bankside Power Station in London, then being considered for what in 2000 would become Tate Modern. After outlining the scope of the building, the brief closed, stating breezily that it was hoped at least part of it would be ready by 1996, when the Northern Region had won the bid to be 'UK Region of the Visual Arts'. The Brief for the competition gave a vivid picture of the very different function of the site at the time, cataloguing its current or recent users: Bridon Ropes factory, Lumsden Machine Company, Jennings Scrap Yard, the Council's 'gypsy caravan site' and the Northern Butchers Hide and Skin depot.

THE WINNING PROPOSAL

140 entries were received for the competition (anonymous throughout its two stages) and on 26 September 1994 the judges awarded Dominic Williams the first prize. The assessors were impressed by the 'very simple approach' of this unknown architect who had only been working for three years, but they were reassured that he had entered with Ellis Williams Architects (his

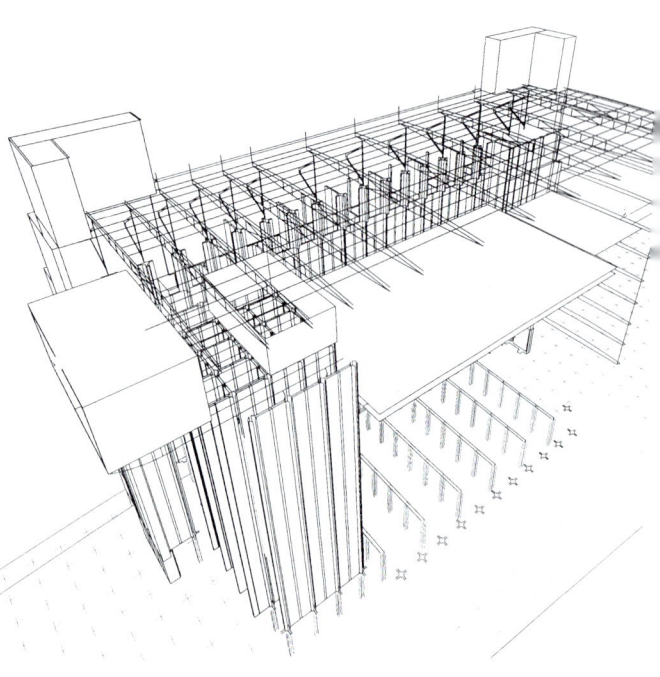

Structural drawing by Dominic Williams prepared as part of Stage 1 of the design competition. It shows the 2.5m grid running throughout and beyond the building and what would become the viewing box on the west (left) side of the building.

Side elevation

father's practice), which had a known track record. The judges felt that his design 'demonstrated a certain poetic quality… and a far greater understanding of the nature of installation art as a form than any other competitor'. Before taking up architecture Williams had completed a one-year foundation course in Fine Art and was indeed very familiar with current contemporary art practice. This identification with the making of the new, combined with a particular sensitivity to the character and nature of the old silo building, informed the project throughout the eight years it took to complete.

Certain key aspects of Williams' proposal for the building remained consistent from his first submission through to the scheme as finally built.

- The building would be emptied of its honeycomb structure of 148 silos, and four main structural floors would be inserted.
- These four main floors would be sub-divided by intermediary floors of lightweight, non-structural and removeable steelwork, providing the building with maximum flexibility to respond to the varying needs of contemporary art practice, which was a keynote of the scheme.
- Visitors would reach the galleries in glass lifts climbing up the west elevation, which would give spectacular views of the Tyne.
- The west and east ends of the building would be largely replaced by glass walls, both to allow natural light into all the floors as well as to emphasise the building's great height.
- A restaurant would be sited on the roof of the building, built in such a way that natural light would still reach the top gallery floor.
- A 'viewing box' protruding prominently from the top

level of the west façade would not only provide spectacular views but would draw attention to the building and orientate it towards the Tyne Bridge and the centres of Newcastle and Gateshead.
• The building's four corner towers, which had been purely cosmetic in the old building, would be made more prominent, with their height increased by the addition of steel 'extensions'.

Although it was clear from the beginning that BALTIC was intended for temporary exhibitions and would not house a permanent collection, the idea that it should be a place where art would be made as well as exhibited came early into the planning and design of the building and of the organisation that would eventually run it. This approach was informed partly by Gateshead's commitment to encouraging participation in the arts and partly by Williams' own interest and experience. It was later enshrined by Sune Nordgren, BALTIC'S first Director, in the phrase 'BALTIC: The Art Factory', where the concept of meeting artists at work as well as seeing their works was promoted as a characteristic to distinguish BALTIC from other centres of contemporary art.

→ Architectural drawing of the west face showing the Riverside Building

With development under way the business case of the BALTIC project received closer scrutiny. It was realised early on that building a bridge across the river in the vicinity of BALTIC would be of benefit: it would provide a connection with the commercial and residential development now gathering pace on the Newcastle side (with its larger population) and would go some way to compensate for the otherwise difficult access to the BALTIC site. Williams sketched a proposal for a bridge in 1995 and this became part of the ongoing negotiation with funders. The concept was finally realised in September 2001 as the Gateshead Millennium Bridge, to the design of Wilkinson Eyre and Partners. The first bridge built across the river at river level since the Swing Bridge in 1876, it became a key link in the regeneration of the riversides of both Newcastle and Gateshead.

LOTTERY SUCCESS

While the Arts Council was considering Gateshead's lottery application for the Baltic building, the North of England was coming to the end of its reign as UK Region of the Visual Arts. Gateshead Council commissioned several works for this festival, including some that took

← *Architectural drawing of the east face with view of rear and riverside*

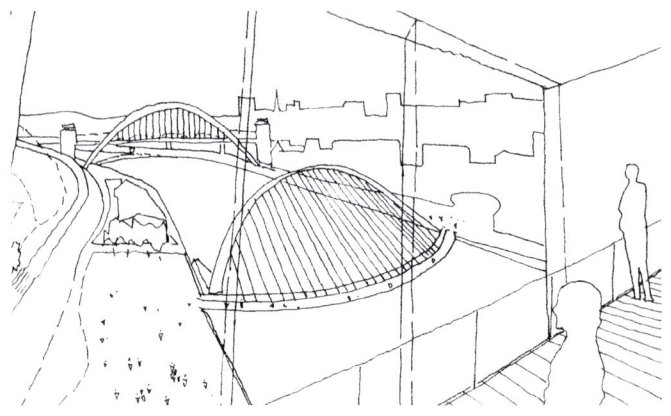

↑ *Architectural drawing of Level 5 Viewing Box.*

place on or around BALTIC, including Jaume Plensa's light beam *Blake in Gateshead*, later re-installed in its current position adjacent to BALTIC's entrance. In the redundant Greenesfield Railway Works, just along the river from Baltic, 25,000 visitors came to see Antony Gormley's *Field for the British Isles*, in the year that Gateshead won £800,000 to commission Gormley to create *The Angel of the North*.

In June 1997 the Arts Council Lottery awarded Gateshead Council a capital grant of £33.4m (towards a total budget of £45.7m) as well as (unusually for the Lottery) £1.5m per year towards the running costs of BALTIC for each of the first five years – just over half of the estimated costs. A condition of this grant was the early appointment of a Director for the project, and in November 1997 Sune Nordgren was appointed as BALTIC's first Director and began the process of finalising the designs for the building and creating the organisation it would house.

THE DEVELOPMENT OF THE DESIGN

At that stage it was planned that entry to the building would be from a large car park to the south, across a bridge that would lead directly into the first floor. As planning guidelines changed (and land values in the vicinity began to increase) the area to the south became the subject of a separate development, initially for shops, housing and a multi-screen cinema but ultimately reduced to apartments only. The entrance was then allocated to the west, and a much reduced car-parking space was moved to the east, where plans for what was to be a performance area were now abandoned.

A one-storey addition to the west of the silo building (the Riverside building) expanded in size and importance as it took over the role of entrance; in addition to the original café bar, a shop and restaurant would also be housed here to help provide additional income for the project. When the final site for the Millennium Bridge was chosen a further building to the west of the bridge (the Smith Print works) was demolished to create more room for what is now Baltic Square, a better connection between the bridge and BALTIC and a kind of performance area to replace the one that had been planned for the east side of the building.

Following a period during which Dominic Williams' original and simple design became increasingly complicated due to the varying demands of a many-headed client, the new Director worked with Williams to return the design to reflect a cleaner and more rational use of space. By pushing plant, storage, escape stairs, staff lifts, the occasional meeting room and toilets into the four corners of the building, the large central area of each floor was freed up to be used as gallery space. Most of the plant required to provide the building with heat and power, air conditioning and distribution was located in a three-storey gas-powered energy centre (one storey of which was underground) created in the car park to the east of the silo building. Of the many consultants who worked on the building the architect had particular praise for Atelier One, the engineers who gave the building its new structural form, and Atelier Ten, the environmental services engineers. Atelier Ten credit Gateshead Council for the extent of their interest (unusual for that time) in finding a sustainable energy strategy for the building.

BALTIC THE ORGANISATION

The concept of BALTIC as an 'art factory', a place where art would be made as well as exhibited, was developed for several reasons. It was in keeping with (and partly emerged from) Gateshead's mission to make contemporary art more accessible; it suited the industrial image of the North East; and, in marketing terms, an art centre of this scale in this location needed its 'unique selling point'. More importantly, Nordgren was convinced that contemporary art could only be understood as process as well as product, and that presentation of contemporary art was enriched by, and in some senses could not be separated from, a process of audience involvement, debate and discussion. BALTIC would therefore be a meeting place, a place of discovery, or for some perhaps simply a place for a coffee, a ride in the lifts and a spectacular view. There was also a belief that to persuade audiences to come and see contemporary art in Gateshead, BALTIC would need, more than big name artists in its shows, the actual presence of working artists; and it would have to provide facilities for the artists to work in as well as good opportunities and support while they were there. Through outreach and education work that became a key part of BALTIC's activity, this residency programme was presented as being beneficial to BALTIC's regional community not just to those who visited the building itself. The other weapon in BALTIC's armoury was its brave policy of 'not taking shows from London [so that] people will come to Gateshead to see things they can't see anywhere else in the UK'. Although this drew the particular ire of art critic Brian Sewell in BALTIC's early years, it has to a remarkable degree remained a consistent policy during the five years of the centre's existence.

THE FINAL REFINEMENT OF THE DESIGN

This 'working' or functionalist curatorial aesthetic drove the development of the design of the building from 1997 through to the form it takes today. In addition to the gradual re-simplification of the spaces and to maintaining maximum flexibility in use and layouts, there was a conscious attempt to avoid creating spaces that would be the classic, bland 'white cubes' so beloved of the

*BALTIC construction
 el 2A, February 2002*

*BALTIC construction,
 ust 2001*

contemporary art gallery. The architecture of each space was allowed to inform the identity of that space as much as possible, with aspects of the old building often being utilised, in the belief that 'artists want to have some kind of challenge with architecture when they create their art' (Sune Nordgren). At the same time the feel and the memory of the old building and its honeycomb of silos was introduced into the new building by keeping the original grid system used for the 148 silos (2.5m x 2.5m) for all the new internal layouts. There was also an honesty in the approach to the materials used. In the sections of the old building that were retained, their materials – predominantly the yellow and red bricks – were honoured and respected, while new parts of the building were expressed in materials that were clearly 'new' – primarily glass, a silvery anodised aluminium and russet-brown Cor-Ten steel.

For ideas on how galleries could work best for contemporary art Dominic Williams spoke to artists and arts organisations throughout the design process. There was a debate about whether, following 'Percent for Art' policy, which was both required under the terms of the Lottery grant and was also Gateshead Council's policy, artists would contribute to the building itself. Wisely, the decision was made not to commission artists to create work as part of the building but to bring the prominent British artist Julian Opie onto the design team before the design had reached its final stages. Williams credits Opie with helping to determine the form and feel of the main spaces, the choice of materials, important details like the junctions between walls and floors, as well as with simplifying the lighting and helping to resolve the form of the new Riverside building. He recalls that Opie was a useful ally, articulating and defending the design aesthetic in meetings between the design team and the client and with other consultants. Opie went on to design a series of temporary works for BALTIC's opening programme, where giant outline figures occupied not only gallery space but also prominent parts of the building itself, and even the Gateshead Millennium Bridge.

BALTIC construction, January 2002

CONSTRUCTION OF THE NEW BALTIC

Converting a 50-metre-high building designed to store grain into a six-floor art centre was a complex and technically challenging job. The first contract was to cut out all the grain silos: this left the 40-metre-high brick facades unsupported, so a special temporary 1,000-tonne steel frame was designed to wrap around and support the whole structure, its weight resting on the building's original foundations. All the materials needed to create the new interior had to be craned in through the top of the building and through this lattice frame.

The four new principal floors were formed from post-tensioned beams cast in situ, tied to the 300mm stubs left over at 2.5 metre centres from where the grain silos connected to the side walls. Additional support for the long floor spans was provided by rows of pillars set out 2.5 metres from the side walls (also following the original grid of silos), the two side aisles that they formed providing the logical route for the main services to the new spaces. The floors can support six-tonne point loadings (i.e. six tonnes at any one particular point). Intermediary floors were constructed with lightweight

← *BALTIC construction, November 1999–June 2000*

↓ *BALTIC construction, May 2000*

BALTIC **17**

BALTIC construction, November 1999–June 2000

steel frames and thin concrete floor-sections, designed to be removeable to adapt spaces in the future.

Ductwork was built into the post-tensioned beams to carry the heated or chilled air supply, which reaches the galleries through diffusers in the floor. More efficient than systems that bring air in from above, this system was unusual in 1994.

INTERIOR DESIGN, MATERIALS AND FURNITURE

The simple, honest, industrial aesthetic developed for the work on the building also extended to the interior design of BALTIC. Apart from glass, concrete and aluminium, the key new materials were: Welsh slate (used throughout the entrance and the floor of the art space on the Ground Floor; Cor-Ten steel, with its distinctive coating of stabilised rust (used for the walls framing the entrance, the interior of the Riverside building and the new top parts of the corners of the building); and a beautiful 150-year-old Swedish pine (used for the floors of all the other galleries and most of the other spaces). This substantial 35mm-thick material gave an appropriate natural and workshop feel and, after much debate, it was decided that the wood should not be given any varnish or surface treatment so that the floors could wear honestly with age and bear the imprint of accumulating years of use.

Most of the furniture for the building – chairs and tables for the café, restaurants, offices and meeting rooms, and storage systems for the offices, archive and bookshop – was commissioned from the Swedish designer Åke Axelsson, designed to be both flexible and durable, and made of a simple range of high-quality materials – pine, aluminium and steel. As was the case for the building itself, the mantra was 'truth to materials': in the original planning, 'nothing is painted, nothing is covered' was the attitude that Sune Nordgren asserted should inform the whole experience of BALTIC.

A WALK THROUGH BALTIC

ARRIVAL

Two imposing walls of Cor-Ten steel frame the entrance: the walls enclose two boxes which contain, on the left, storage for BALTIC Shop and, on the right, storage for the Café Bar. The back wall of the Café Bar is a continuation of the retaining wall of thin slices of slate on the square outside, onto which the Café Bar spills out. The Café Bar's tables and chairs are part of the original furniture designed for BALTIC by Åke Axelsson, although the storage system originally designed for the shop is no longer in use.

Under a glass roof which allows light to pour in, two flights of stairs – only 12 steps in all – lead gently up to the main building. This extension is known as the 'Riverside' and looking up through the roof, the west wall of the main building and three glass scenic lifts for transporting visitors can be seen. This extension clearly separates the old from the new and the architect fought hard to keep it low so that it did not detract from the original building. The whole of this entrance area is now used as a small exhibition space and is known as 'The Street'.

BALTIC Café Bar

Staircase inside the main entrance to BALTIC

Mark Titchner's 2007 installation **The Future is Behind Us**, in The Street

← *Installation view of **Just Kidding: Time is the Enemy** by Dzine, 2006*

→ *BALTIC Café Bar, with the original furniture designed by Åke Axelsson*

→ The Riverside space and terrace

↑ The information desk, designed by Holmes-Wood and staffed by BALTIC Crew

→ BALTIC Shop, located in the Riverside Building and designed by Kit Grover

GROUND FLOOR

As you reach the top of the stairs, to your left, through the glass doorway, is Jaume Plensa's lightbeam, entitled *Blake in Gateshead*. Behind here, stairs lead to the Riverside Space, which is used for dining and events and spills out onto a terrace looking north over the Tyne. Directly behind the information desk are the scenic lifts which take visitors to the main exhibition spaces. Beyond the lifts lies the Ground Floor gallery.

All the floors of the Riverside building are slate, and this material continues through the Ground Floor gallery. Beyond this space are artists' studios, workshops, exhibition storage and, through a demountable partition in the back wall, the loading area where full-size trucks can drive in and off-load directly into the building.

Getting around BALTIC is both easy and challenging at the same time. In all, there are 13 separate levels in the building; the architect himself said that he wanted to produce some sense of disorientation because it was good for a building to generate a sense of discovery. The scenic lifts stop at every main floor but there are six

← Architectural drawing of the Ground Floor

↓ Jaume Plensa's permanent light beam installation, **Blake in Gateshead**

additional intermediary floors (mainly for use by staff). Through the glass wall to your left, as you stand facing the lifts, is the public stairwell. The stairs are simple – industrial steel-plate flooring and perforated steel balustrades. Slightly dark at first, the upper reaches are naturally lit through glass bricks fitted into slots in the external walls.

↑ **Neon Circle** (2001), Ground Floor installation by Carsten Höller which formed part of the opening programme

→ Ground Floor art space

Public stairwell leading all of the main levels

The stairwell is also occasionally used as an alternative exhibition space. Installation: Graham Dolphin, *Repeater* (2007)

← *Installation view of Fabien Verschaere exhibition* **After Seven Remix** *(2007)*

→ *Installation view of Surasi Kusolwong exhibition* **Woman, machine, motion** *(2006)*

LEVEL 1

A big number '1' in BALTIC's distinctive typeface marks your arrival at the top of the stairs at Level 1. If the lift stops and the door is open (this floor is not always in use), look up from the generous space outside the lifts (every main floor has such an 'orientation space') and you will see the intermediary floor inserted above. Ahead of you a corridor leads to a large flexible space at the other end of the building which is fully equipped for films, performance and lectures, and is lit by the huge glass window in the east wall, or completely blacked out. Projection rooms and storage and control areas look down on this space from the mezzanine floor above. Media labs for artists working in sound or film used to take up the remainder of this level but they have recently been converted into staff rooms.

Either side of the corridor approaching this space are two acoustically self-contained areas: to the left is a small black cinema or lecture space, with retractable seating for 60, and to the right, an identically sized white space named the 'Cave' on the architect's plans. With part of its floor removeable, the original idea for this space was that it could be used for 360-degree 'virtual reality' projections.

↑ Installation view of Marcus Coates exhibition **Dawn Chorus** (2007)

→ Installation view of Graham Dolphin exhibition **Repeater** (2007)

← Installation view of Whiteplanes exhibition ***Whiteplane 2*** (2005)

→ Installation view of Bob & Roberta Smith exhibition ***Help Build the Ruins of Democracy*** (2004)

LEVEL 2

Stepping out of the lift, a high gallery space extends out in front and another mezzanine floor containing glass-walled offices is set to the right and left above. From here it is possible for the first time to get a view right through the building to the east wall. As you continue through the space, you will note a spiral staircase which allows staff to reach the open-plan office area directly above. Glass walls allow you to see to the left and right, with the prominent Library and Archive on the right, where the life of BALTIC is documented in images, publications, reviews and press cuttings and informed by an impressive library of catalogues and books. Much of this material is accessible through BALTIC's web site but physical access to the archive and library can be arranged by appointment.

Until 2007 you could look into the open area at the east end of this floor and see BALTIC's staff relaxing in their break time. In one of the few changes to the layout of the building this area (Quay) is now used for formal and informal education activities, and the staff now relaxes unseen by the public on Level 1A.

Installation view of
arnaby Furnas exhibition
ecent Paintings (2005)

Installation view of
oseph Havel exhibition
ght (2007)

← Inside BALTIC's Library & Archive, open by appointment to the public

→ View into the Information Superhighway studio. The vinyl drawings in this space are by Yoshitomo Nara.

← The east facing window at the rear of BALTIC (vinyl drawing by Yoshitomo Nara)

→ View into Quay, BALTIC's drop-in learning area where events and activities take place

OVERLEAF
Left: View into Quay lounge with plasma screens
Right: View into Quay, complete with boat where storytelling takes place

View into Quay studio, used for workshops and activities (vinyl drawings by Yoshitomo Nara)

LEVEL 3

The largest space in BALTIC, Level 3 is also the building's most advanced in terms of its environmental conditions. Levels of light, humidity and temperature can be controlled to museum conditions for particularly sensitive displays. Notice the slots in the pine floor from where the air systems are diffused. At the back of the gallery, the big Teflon 'sail', which is pulled across by hand, might be drawn across the east window, softening the incoming light. On the left at the back of this gallery, behind folding doors, is BALTIC's substantial art lift. Accessed either from inside the building or directly from outside, on the Ground Floor, it delivers artworks to Levels 1, 2, 3 and 4.

By now you will have seen or been spoken to by a member of the BALTIC Crew. Clearly identifiable by their T-shirts, they share a number of roles in BALTIC, and with many of them practising artists, it can be particularly useful to discuss what is on show with them.

← *Installation view of Susan Hiller exhibit* **Witness** *(2004)*

→ *View of Level 3 featuring Kienholz retrospective exhibition and, in the foregroun the artwork* **My Country Tis of Thee** *(200*

← Installation view of Ed Kienholz exhibit **The Big Double Cross** (2005)

→ Installation view of Zabludowicz Collection exhibition **When We Build, Let Us Think That We Build Forever** (2007)

LEVEL 4

Part of what was first thought to make the Baltic building unsuitable for use as an art centre – its narrowness and its height – in fact provides BALTIC with one of its most exciting features. Each floor becomes progressively lighter as you make your way up through the building until, when you reach the top gallery on Level 4, the light pours in through the glass roof-sections (unless the gallery has been blacked out for an exhibition, with specially fitted blinds). There is in fact another floor above this: the ceiling of this gallery is the floor of the Rooftop Restaurant. Through the glass roof you can see the diagonal struts which carry its weight. This is a good place to see the Cor-Ten steel corner towers which were added to the original building to contain service plant and which emphasise the corners of the new building.

A door on the north side of the building on Level 4 leads out onto the Viewing Terrace, giving fantastic views up and down the river Tyne. The terrace sits on the roof of the Receiving House, a section of the building projecting over the riverside where the grain was 'received' from the ships before passing into the silos. Into this space the architect stacked six good-sized work areas and meeting rooms accessible from the main or mezzanine floors of the main building. The old window lines of this block were run together with continuous vertical ribbons of glass, clearly exposing the new levels and expressing the new function of this otherwise ordinary excrescence. This can be seen best from the Millennium Bridge.

↑ *Level 4 Viewing Terrace overlooking the River Tyne*

→ *Installation view of Ed Kien* exhibits: **The Caddy Court, The Ozymandias Parade** and **The Go-World or Begat By Chanc The Wonder Horse Trigger** (2

← Installation view of Phyllida Barlow exhibition ***Peninsula*** (2005)

→ Installation view of Antony Gormley exhibition ***Domain Field*** (2003)

↑ Level 4 art space

← Installation view of the exhibition **Spank the Monkey** (2006)

BALTIC 55

LEVEL 5

Overlooking the Level 4 gallery is a viewing gallery reached from Level 5. Apart from the delight of looking down onto this large space, you can watch the 'Art Factory' at work from this vantage point, where artists and technicians might be installing or sometimes making work for an exhibition on Level 4. It was from this viewing gallery during four months of 2003 that visitors could look down on the spectacle of 286 volunteers having their

Invader exhibit on Level 5 Viewing Box, part of the **Spank the Monkey** exhibition (2006)

The view from Level 5 Viewing Box over the River Tyne and the Quayside bodies moulded in plaster for Antony Gormley's *Domain Field*.

Heading in the opposite direction from this viewing gallery leads to the Viewing Box. Projecting out above the entrance to the building, this is one of the most distinctive features of BALTIC's exterior, and one of the most popular interior features. Encased in aluminium with a glass end wall, it was a key feature of Dominic Williams' original design for the 1994 competition. It is in fact a two-level box, the top level being reached from the Rooftop Restaurant on Level 6. The glass screen separating the two levels was fitted later to prevent sound travelling from the public gallery up to the restaurant and vice-versa.

LEVEL 6

With stunning 360-degree views, the Rooftop Restaurant is the culmination of the BALTIC journey, where the architect's use of glass and appreciation of BALTIC's spectacular location is clearly evidenced. Even washing your hands in the ladies toilets offers a view east down the Tyne through a floor-to-ceiling glass wall which is 42 metres above the ground.

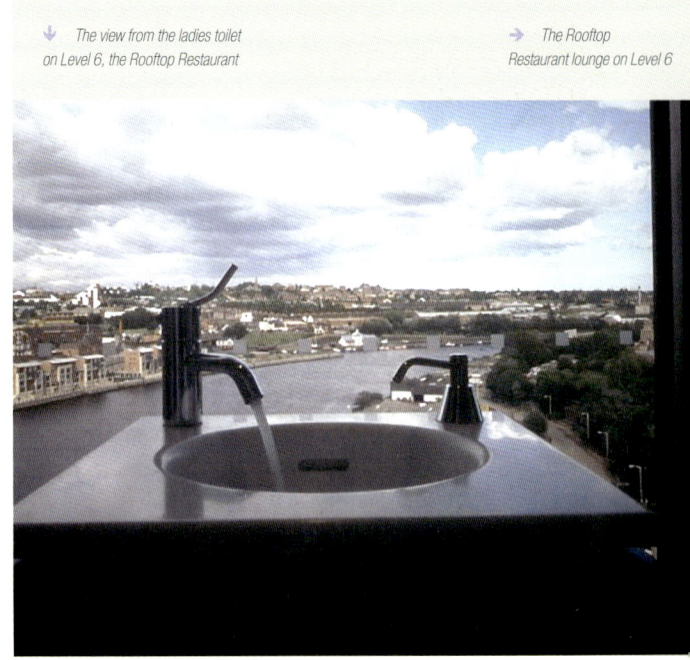

↓ The view from the ladies toilet on Level 6, the Rooftop Restaurant

→ The Rooftop Restaurant lounge on Level 6

THE PRE-OPENING PROGRAMME
1999–2002

Construction of the new BALTIC took nearly four years, during which time the organisation began to introduce itself to the North East and to the international art world with a bold programme of artists in residence, exhibitions, installations, publications and events taking place in and around Gateshead and Newcastle, as well as further afield. Two of these in particular drew the attention of large outside audiences to BALTIC's future potential. Between July and September 1999, in the phase between the demolition of the honeycomb core of the old building and the insertion of the new floors, the artist Anish Kapoor strung out his work, *Taratantara*, in the newly exposed vast interior void of the building's shell. Injecting the building with bright red new life, this event marked the definitive boundary between the building's old life and its new incarnation, and brought 16,000 people to the BALTIC site. A year later, in October 2000, Jenny Holzer's *Truisms* were projected across the Tyne onto the entire 40-metre-high north face of the building.

This programme, along with the building's progress and the development of the emerging organisation that was BALTIC were documented and promoted in the distinctive BALTIC newsletters, sixteen now much-collected issues published between October 1998 and the opening in July 2002. In their distinctive 340 mm x 480 mm format, printed in black on newsprint paper, these newsletters designed by the Gateshead-based design consultancy Ripe began to form BALTIC's public image, carrying the simple industrial aesthetic into the medium of print and communication.

An important part of this image, used first in these newsletters but ultimately in all BALTIC branding and promotion, was the BALTIC typeface. Not dissimilar to the giant ceramic lettering that spelt out BALTIC FLOUR MILLS and JOSEPH RANK LIMITED on either side of the old building, the typeface and graphic style, based on a 1940s design and produced by two Swedish designers, Ulf Greger Nilsson and Henrik Nygren, was further developed by BALTIC and Ripe Design. It is now a registered typeface called BALTIC Affisch.

Anish Kapoor installation Taratantara (1999)

B. OPEN

BALTIC opened to the public at one minute past midnight on 13 July 2002. Its first exhibition, 'B.Open' was designed both to show the full potential of the new building and to make manifest the concept of an 'Art Factory'. The multipurpose space on Level 1 was used for the installation of *Dream Time*, a multiscreen film by Jane and Louise Wilson not shown before in the UK. Jaume Plensa complemented *Blake in Gateshead* with a series of benches for peaceful viewing around the building, and made a new installation of nine pairs of gongs on Level 3. Looking out onto the Tyne Bridge from Level 4 was a 1/20th-size model of the Tyne Bridge made out of Meccano by Chris Burden. Celebrating BALTIC's past, bread was a theme for live art during the opening weekend, with Tatsumi Orimito's *Bread Man* procession and Anne Bjerge Hansen's all-day *Moving Bakery*, which dispensed bread to passers by in Baltic Square.

BALTIC was visited by one million people in its first year.

← *Projection on the north face announcing the opening date of BALTIC*

→ *BALTIC from the east face (rear,*

© Scala Publishers Ltd, 2008
Text © Andrew Guest, Director of Northern Architecture – the architecture centre for the North East of England

First published in 2008 by Scala Publishers Ltd in association with BALTIC

Scala Publishers Ltd
Northburgh House
10 Northburgh Street
London EC1V 0AT
www.scalapublishers.com

ISBN 978 1 85759 445 4

Edited by Sandra Pisano
Designed by Nigel Soper
Printed in China

10 9 8 7 6 5 4 3 2 1

All rights reserved. No part of this book may be reproduced, stored in a retrieval system or transmitted in any form or by any means electronic, mechanical, photocopying, recording or otherwise, without the written permission of Scala Publishers Ltd.

Every effort has been made to acknowledge correct copyright of images where applicable. Any errors or omissions are unintentional and should be notified to the publishers.

Front cover: BALTIC viewed from Newcastle Quayside with Gateshead Millennium Bridge in foreground
Back cover: BALTIC and Jaume Plensa's light beam installation, *Blake in Gateshead*
Page 1: BALTIC viewed from Newcastle Quayside

ACKNOWLEDGEMENTS
The author would like to thank the following: Gary Malkin, Sara Ley, Craig Astley and Jason Allan of BALTIC, Dominic Williams, Dennis Robson.

BIBLIOGRAPHY
In its short life, BALTIC has already published much about itself. These are the main sources useful for the story of its genesis and the development of the building.
BALTIC: The Art Factory, BALTIC Centre for Contemporary Art, 2002
B.HERE, BALTIC Centre for Contemporary Art, 2002
B.YEAR ONE, BALTIC Centre for Contemporary Art, 2003
B.READ/ONE: New Sites - New Art, BALTIC Centre for Contemporary Art, 2000
B.INFO, BALTIC Centre for Contemporary Art, 2003

PHOTOGRAPHY CREDITS
BALTIC © BALTIC (pp 14-18); Neville Blaszk © Carsten Höller (p 27 [left]); Bonney's Newsagency © Bonney's Newsagency (p 62); Critical Tortoise © BALTIC (pp 21 [top], 23, 24, 25 [left], 57, 59, 63); Colin Davison © BALTIC (front cover, pp 1, 2, 3, 20, 25 [right], 28, 38, 40, 41, 42, 43, 44, 45); Colin Davison © BALTIC/Phyllida Barlow (p 52); Colin Davison © BALTIC/Marcus Coates (p 32); Colin Davison © BALTIC/Graham Dolphin (p 33); Colin Davison © BALTIC/Barnaby Furnas (p 36); Colin Davison © BALTIC/Antony Gormley (p 53); Colin Davison © BALTIC/Joseph Havel (p 37); Colin Davison © BALTIC/Susan Hiller (p 46); Colin Davison © BALTIC/Surasi Kusolwong (p 31); Colin Davison © BALTIC/Bob & Roberta Smith (p 35); Colin Davison © BALTIC/Spank the Monkey (pp54-55, 56); Colin Davison © BALTIC/Fabien Verschaere (p 30); Colin Davison © BALTIC/Whiteplanes (p 34); Colin Davison © BALTIC/Zabludowicz Collection artists (p 49); Colin Davison © Graham Dolphin (p 29); Colin Davison © BALTIC © Mark Titchner (p 21 [bottom]); Colin Davison © Dzine (p 22); Colin Davison © Nancy Reddin Kienholz (pp 47, 48, 51); Doug Hall © BALTIC (p 50); Jerry Hardman-Jones © BALTIC (back cover); Jerry Hardman-Jones © Jaume Plensa (p 26 [right]); photograph courtesy of Rank Hovis McDougall (p 5); John Riddy © BALTIC (pp 7, 27 [right], 55, 58); John Riddy © BALTIC/Anish Kapoor (p 60); Robert Straughton © Robert Straughton/Rookhow Photographic (p 4); James Tolley © BALTIC (p 39); Dominic Williams, Ellis Williams Architects © Ellis Williams Architects, London (pp 8-12, 26 [left]).